6.50

D1559848

Prayer-poems to nourish the Spirit

WHEN *the* BLUE HERON FLIES

MELANNIE SVOBODA, SND

Foreword by Robert F. Morneau

TWENTY
THIRD 23rd
PUBLICATIONS
NEW LONDON, CT 06320
WWW.23RDPUBLICATIONS.COM

TWENTY-THIRD PUBLICATIONS
A Division of Bayard
One Montauk Avenue, Suite 200
New London, CT 06320
(860) 437-3012 or (800) 321-0411
www.23rdpublications.com

Cover image © iStockphotos.com / Visions by Atlee

Library of Congress Cataloging-in-Publication Data

Svoboda, Melannie.
    When the blue heron flies : prayer-poems to nourish the spirit / Melannie Svoboda.
        p. cm.
    Includes index.
    ISBN 978-1-58595-866-5
    1. Meditations. 2. Catholic Church--Prayers and devotions. I. Title.
BX2182.3.S89 2012
242--dc23
                            2012007468

ISBN 978-1-58595-866-5
Printed in the U.S.A.

DEDICATION

*To Father Demetrius Dumm, OSB
my teacher, mentor, friend*

CONTENTS

FOREWORD

One of the greatest imperatives in life is simply this: "Be attentive." When that attention is coupled with love, we enter the field of contemplation: loving attention. The philosophers taught us that every being has some components of truth, goodness, and beauty. Thus, by paying attention to whatever crosses our path, we have the opportunity to encounter the mystery of God, the source of all life and holiness, the source of all truth, goodness, and beauty.

Sr. Melannie Svoboda is a "noticer." She was probably born with "n.b." tattooed on her heart: *nota bene*, note well. In this book she ponders the tilt of the earth, skunks and blue herons, her mother's yellow jacket, biblical figures like Bartimaeus, Habakkuk, and the Magi, the experiences of homesickness and perfectionism, the nature of grief and space. Along with this noticing is a deep love for words. Indeed, Sr. Melannie identifies herself as a "Wooer of Words." She has that graced obsession of translating experiences and feelings into images and concepts lest the experiences are forever forgotten.

A unique feature of this volume is that each poetic expression is followed by a brief reflection, some suggested Scripture passages, and questions that hopefully lead to prayer and play. An index of Scripture references, topics, and themes also makes the book very user friendly.

Sr. Melannie's playfulness and humor permeate these pages. In contrast to Hopkins' "The world is charged with the grandeur of God," she suggests that the world is charged with the snares of God; after reading *Moby Dick*, she was hoping that Melville would let a whale be a whale and not some great philosophical metaphor; when pondering the vastness of the universe, she deduced its size as the Creator's fondness for elbowroom; even the serpent in paradise, like Adam and Eve, refused responsibility for his trickery because of an abusive father, a neglectful mother. But along with this sense of play is a poignancy that runs deep as she speaks about the death of her father and the trials of her friend's Uncle Joe.

While entertaining, this book has a strong educational component. We are given advice on how to embrace ambiguity, on how to see sacredness in every encounter, on appreciating that heaven is closer than we thought. But these teachings are indirect, offered to us through symbols and stories. And for that, she deserves our gratitude.

Ralph Waldo Emerson states: "The poet is the sayer, the namer, and represents beauty." It was way back in Eden that Adam began the naming process, and it continues in our day. Sr. Melannie is part of that lineage, and we are the beneficiaries.

Bishop Robert F. Morneau
Green Bay, Wisconsin

INTRODUCTION

A blue heron lives near me. (Strictly speaking he is a Great Blue Heron, *ardea herodias*.) Sometimes I see him wading in the water's edge of a nearby lake. He stands motionless on his long, stately legs, fishing. Often he blends in so well with the tall grasses and reeds that I don't notice him until he stirs at my approach or springs out of the water and flies away.

And how he can fly! Blue herons fly very gracefully with a deep, slow beating of their large wings. They hold their necks in an "S" curve in flight with their long legs stretched out straight behind them. At nearly four feet tall, the blue heron is an impressive figure, whether flying majestically high across the sky, walking erect with long strides along the shore, or standing fixedly in shallow water.

Coming upon the blue heron always delights me. More than that, it stops me in my tracks, giving me pause. Sometimes it even elicits an audible "Ah!" or "Wow!" from me. But most of all the blue heron reaffirms for me the profound mystery and beauty of everyday existence.

I entitled this book *When the Blue Heron Flies* because I hope these simple poems (in some small way) will do for you what the blue heron does for me. I hope they will pique your curiosity, slow you down, and reaffirm for you the mystery and beauty of daily life with its light and shadows, joys and sorrows, perplexities and understanding. I also hope these poems will nudge you to prayer.

The blue heron is a magnificent bird, a veritable "poem in motion." He makes me wonder, What must the Creator be like? May the poems in this book attune you more and more to the poetry of your own particular life. And may they lead you ever closer to the Creator of us all.

1. Ambiguity

Learn to live with ambiguity,
  with blurred lines, fuzzy edges,
fluid seams where one thing
  spills into its opposite.
Be patient with all
  that is uncertain in your life.
Enjoy mixtures,
  befriend apparent contradictions,
don't be in such a rush
  to get closure every time.

Whoever said life was meant to be
  one, pure, whole, and graspable?

And if by chance you spot
  a little certainty fluttering nearby,
don't reach out for her
and clasp her madly to your chest
or hoist her high above your head
  like some tin trophy
or wield her like a club to force submission.

Instead, allow her to alight on the palm
  of your open and trembling hand.

The writer Elie Wiesel once said, "A fanatic has the answer before he has the question. In fact, he has no questions." This poem celebrates the questions and ambiguity in our daily lives. It reminds us that life comes to us not as "pure" and "whole," but as "mixtures" and "apparent contradictions"—like the weeds and wheat in Jesus' parable. Those who claim to have found "the truth" can be dangerous, as this poem suggests. In Psalm 55 God says to us, "As high as the heavens are above the earth, so high are my ways above your ways and my thoughts above your thoughts." We must remember that Truth is but another name for our fathomless God.

For reflection

1. Reflect on some of the "blurred lines" and "fuzzy edges" you have experienced in life. What helps you to deal with them?

2. How do you reconcile the Church's teachings or dogmas with this poem celebrating ambiguity?

Suggested Scripture

ISAIAH 55
An invitation to seek God

MATTHEW 13:24–30
The parable of the weeds among the wheat

For prayer and play

This poem compares "a little certainty" to a butterfly. Can you come up with some other images of certainty or truth? Or write a prayer or poem that addresses God as Truth.

2. Ask not why

Ask not why the young mother
  rocks her ailing child
    through the long, dark night;
nor try to figure out
why the firefighter
  ran into the burning house
    to save the elderly man.

Ask not why the father
  toils in the deep coal mine,
    and sees the sun only on Sundays;
nor try to make sense of
the young man's need
  to sit at the bedside
    of his comatose grandfather.

Ask not why the teacher
  works with students
    others label unreachable;
nor try to fathom
how that couple,
  after fifty years of marriage,
    can still hold hands.

Ask not why the cloistered nun
  prays in the small, bare chapel
    for a world she has,
      in one way, left;
nor try to understand
why the seamstress
  left a small fortune in her will
    for college students
      she will never know.

Ask not why,
  for there is no reasonable answer.
There is only humanity
  at its best: loving.

Every day we come across stories of ordinary individuals doing extraordinary things. Sometimes these stories are buried in the back pages of our newspapers or stuck at the end of a newscast. But the stories are there—if we look for them. This poem is based on stories of real people who make me proud to be a part of humanity.

For reflection

1. Do any of the stories in this poem touch you? If so, which one(s) and why?

2. Can you think of other stories that demonstrate "humanity at its best: loving"?

Suggested Scripture

GENESIS 18:1–15
   Abraham's visitors

MARK 14:3–9
   The anointing at Bethany

For prayer and play

Read prayerfully the account of Abraham's visitors. If you followed Abraham's beautiful example of hospitality in your current situation, how would you welcome these guests?

   Or read prayerfully the story of the anointing at Bethany. Pretend you are the woman. How would you feel about what you did for Jesus and what he said about you?

3. Babies are a good idea

Babies are a good idea.
That we do not start out in life fully grown
   (as Athena did from Zeus' head),
but rather come into this world
   tiny, wet, and wiggling
with only two skills: crying and sucking—
this is a very good idea.

Babies need someone else to care for them
   twenty-four hours a day.
They need to be fed, changed,
   bathed, held, and gently rocked.
Babies force us to slow down.
They elicit "oohs" and "aahs."

They cause dignified adults
   to make funny faces, talk gibberish,
      and get down on all fours.

Babies call forth from us
   thoughtfulness and tenderness.
But most of all they inspire us to hope
   for a better world—
and to work to make that world a reality.

Someone has said, "The great events of this world are not battles and elections and earthquakes and thunderbolts. The great events are babies, for each child comes with a message that God is not yet discouraged with humanity but is still expecting goodwill to become incarnate in each human life." Babies also afford the rest of us countless opportunities to love. Their big eyes, tiny feet, and inquisitive facial expressions all elicit a tenderness from us we might otherwise not have known we possessed.

For reflection

1. Recall some of the positive experiences you have had with babies or small children. Do you think babies "force us to slow down" and "call forth thoughtfulness and tenderness" from us?

2. What are some ways you are working to make this world a better place for future generations? What else could you do?

Suggested Scripture

LUKE 2:1–20
 The birth of Jesus

MARK 10:13–16
 Jesus and the little children

For prayer and play

Observe or play with a baby or small child today. Or study some pictures of babies—maybe from your family photo album. Notice the effect that these babies' faces and actions have on you. Or read prayerfully the story of Jesus' birth—even if it's not Christmas! What details in the story strike you? Dialog with Jesus about his becoming a baby.

4. Bartimaeus

Questions for myself
upon reading the story
  of Bartimaeus:

He created a scene,
  he made a big fuss.
Is my prayer too mannerly,
  my pleading too decorous?

He threw off his cloak,
he jumped up and came.
What must I surrender
  when Jesus calls my name?

He said, "Master, I want to see."
Can I express my deepest needs
  so simply and readily?

He followed Jesus on the way.
How will I follow Jesus today?

Bartimaeus was a blind beggar who happens to be by the side of the road as Jesus is leaving Jericho with "a sizeable crowd." When he hears it is Jesus of Nazareth who is passing by, he cries out, "Jesus, son of David, have pity on me." People in the crowd try to quiet him. After all, he is creating a scene. But the more they try to shush him, the louder he yells. By doing so, he gets Jesus' attention and is eventually cured because of his faith. Bartimaeus reminds us that, when our need is great, we can throw decorum aside. When our faith is great, we will see in new ways.

For reflection

1. Is your prayer too mannerly, too decorous? If so, what is holding you back from expressing your deepest needs to God?

2. What things do you have to surrender right now in your life in order to respond more fully to the call of Jesus? (Hint: they may not be "things.")

Suggested Scripture

PSALM 6
 A prayer in distress

MARK 10:46–52
 The cure of Bartimaeus

For prayer and play

Bartimaeus is being interviewed by a local newspaper reporter after being cured. Write the reporter's questions and Bartimaeus' answers. Or write a prayer in distress similar to Psalm 6 and similar to Bartimaeus' pleadings.

5. The Beatific Vision

"The contemplation of God in Heavenly Glory"
(Catechism of the Catholic Church)

What if it doesn't mean
   the Thing Seen,
God in Resplendent Glory,
but rather
   the act of seeing—
seeing everything
   as God sees?

Then what?

When I was a child, I was taught that the Beatific Vision was what we "saw" when we got to heaven. It was God sitting in regal majesty upon his throne. Recently I heard Father Michael Himes present another way of looking at that phrase.

For reflection

1. What is your understanding of the phrase "The Beatific Vision"?

2. How do you answer the questions posed in this poem?

Suggested Scripture

ISAIAH 65:17–25
The world renewed

REVELATION 21:1–4
The new heaven and new earth

For prayer and play

After reflecting on the two Scripture passages, write a brief essay entitled "Heaven According to Me." Or write a letter to a child, telling what heaven will be like.

6. The bent woman

She has no name.
But when you are as bent
  as a candy cane,
your identity is easily reduced
  to your infirmity:
  bent woman.

And you are clumsy, slow moving,
  and in great, great pain.
And all you can see
is the little patch of ground
  around your feet.

Such a condition
  (over eighteen years no less!)
makes you prone
  to isolation and hopelessness.
Yet, there she is in the synagogue
  that Sabbath day,
worshiping with all the rest
who stand straight and tall.

And when Jesus summons her,
   she comes.
And when he lays his hands upon her,
   she stands erect.
And when she realizes she is cured,
   she glorifies God.

Then Jesus has to defend his healing
   to a huffy synagogue ruler—
for whom the woman's pain
   was theoretical and inconvenient.

But Jesus, for whom bentness
   is always real and urgent, cries out,
"People are more sacred than law!"
And, "Compassion doesn't know
   what day of the week it is!"

The writer Flannery O'Connor, who died of the crippling disease systemic lupus before her fortieth birthday, wrote this to a friend: "In a sense, sickness is a place, more instructive than a trip to Europe. It's always a place where there's no company, where nobody can follow." The brief account of the cure of the bent woman demonstrates Jesus' sensitivity to sickness. He goes where pain is. Despite the large crowd, he notices the woman. Though she herself never asks for a cure, he invites her to come forward. He lays his hands upon her, unbending the curvature of her spine and restoring her dignity as a "Daughter of Abraham."

For reflection

1. Do you ever reduce people to their "infirmity"? Do you ever find yourself saying or thinking things like this: that ill old man, ungrateful son, cantankerous woman, smart-mouthed teenager, nosy neighbor, cheating husband, etc.? What can help you to see individuals in a more positive and holistic light?

2. Jesus freed the woman of her infirmity. If Jesus called you over today, what would he want to free you of?

Suggested Scripture

LUKE 13:10–17
   Cure of the bent woman

LUKE 14:1–6
   Cure of the man with dropsy

For prayer and play

Read prayerfully the two accounts in Luke. What similarities do you find? What differences? Or write a prayer or poem that begins with, "Free me, Jesus."

7. The blue heron

At the edge of the lake
the blue heron stands motionless
  on stately legs.
Poised. Waiting.
In a flash he pierces the water
with his sharp beak,
  catching a small fish.
Throwing back his head
he lets the fish slide whole
  down his elegant throat.

All the while he fishes,
he eyes the man with pole and line
  planted on the other shore.

Later back at his nest,
the heron tells his wife:
  "Poor humans!
    They have two stumps for legs,
    no neck to speak of,
      and they're totally beakless.
  What a pity!"

Sometimes I envy certain animals: the cheetah for its speed, the eagle for its soaring, the rabbit for its soft fur, the dolphin for its sleekness. We humans traditionally have thought of ourselves as the superior animal because of our larger brains and intellectual capacity. But let us not forget to notice and appreciate the beauty, skills, and ingenuity of our fellow animals.

For reflection

1. This poem captures the thoughts of the heron upon noticing the fisherman across the lake. What might be the fisherman's thoughts about the heron?

2. What aspects of certain birds or animals do you notice and admire?

Suggested Scripture

GENESIS 1:20–31
Fifth and sixth day of creation

PSALM 96
Praise to the God of the universe

For prayer and play

Page through one of the gospels today and note Jesus' use of animals in his teachings and parables—for example, birds, sheep, goats, snakes, camels. How effective are his images? Or choose an animal (besides the heron!) and imagine what this particular animal might say about human beings.

8. Courage

Courage is a crocus
  pushing up through the snow.
Courage is a firefly
  blinking a soft glow.

Courage is a blossom
  swaying in the storm.
Courage is a robin
  chirping in the morn.

Courage is a gosling
  breaking through its shell.
Courage is a hermit
  praying in his cell.

Courage is a sentry
  standing in the night.
Courage is anyone
  doing what is right.

We sometimes think courage is reserved for battlefields, courtrooms, and athletic fields. But there are many other examples of courage that often go unnoticed. This poem celebrates some of them.

For reflection

1. In what way is each example in the poem a kind of courage?

2. What other examples of courage can you think of?

Suggested Scripture

ESTHER 4, CH. C 12–30
Prayer of Queen Esther

ACTS 7:54–60
Martyrdom of Stephen

For prayer and play

Read prayerfully the prayer of Queen Esther and the martyrdom of St. Stephen. How did each of them show great courage? What do their words reveal about the source of their courage? Or reflect on a time you yourself had to have courage. What were the circumstances? What was challenging for you? How did you show courage? What helped you to do so? Was prayer a major factor in this incident?

9. Don't see all you see

"Don't see all you see.
  Don't hear all you hear."

Learn the gentle art of overlooking.
Learn when to pay attention
  and when to look the other way.
Learn which words to heed,
  and which to forget.

Look at it this way:
Do you want others
to note your every misdeed,
  to dwell upon your every slip?
Do you want them to carve in stone
your thoughtless remarks,
  your unkind words?

I didn't think so.
Then for heaven's sake,
cut the slack for others
  you wish them to cut for you.
Remember: overlooking
  can be a form of forgiveness.

I came across this proverb (the first two lines of the poem) many years ago when I was teaching high school. I thought it was a good proverb for teachers to live by. Now I believe it is a good proverb for everyone.

For reflection

1. How do we know when to pay attention and when to overlook?

2. Do you personally agree with the last two lines of the poem? Why or why not?

Suggested Scripture

PSALM 86
Prayer in distress

MATTHEW 7:1–5
Do not judge

For prayer and play

Reflect on these quotations about forgiveness. Then add your own.

* *"To forgive is to set a prisoner free and to discover the prisoner was* you." (Anonymous)

* *"The chance to begin again is one of God's greatest graces."* (Joan Chittister, OSB)

* *"Forgiveness is having given up all hope of having had a better past."* (Anne Lamott)

* *"Forgiveness is the beginning, the middle, and the end of gospel life."* (Fr. Richard Rohr)

10. Earth tilts

Earth tilts on her axis.
Like a little old lady,
she leans slightly to one side.
This apparent defect
   is fortuitous blessing for us,
causing (in much of the world)
our four seasons:
   lengthening sunny days,
   blazing orange maples,
   cascading snowflakes,
   and green shoots of who-knows-what
      pushing up through thick mud.

Would that every tilt
   would yield such bounty.

Imperfections and shortcomings can be blessings in disguise. The boy, too short and small for most sports, becomes an Olympic gold medal ice-skater. The young man crippled by polio develops interior strengths and goes on to be a great president of the United States. The woman whose sister was mentally challenged starts an international movement called the Special Olympics. Some "tilts" yield a rich bounty.

For reflection

1. What other examples can you think of where an apparent imperfection or a negative experience turned out to be a blessing?

2. How attentive are you to the changing of the seasons wherever you live? What possible spiritual benefits can there be in being attentive to the various seasons?

Suggested Scripture

1 SAMUEL 17:32–51
  David fights Goliath

2 CORINTHIANS 12:7–9
  Paul boasts of his weakness

For prayer and play

Write a prayer of thanksgiving for one of the seasons—or for all four. Or reflect on where you are interiorly right now in your life. Which season are you experiencing? Why do you think so?

11. Every act

Your every act should be done in love.
(1 Corinthians 16:14)

Every act?

You mean folding socks, trimming bushes,
    driving to work, standing in line,
tying shoes, feeding the cat,
    texting a friend, attending a meeting,
taking a shower, answering the phone,
    changing a diaper, surfing the Web,
working a lathe, napping on the couch,
    jogging in the park, making a donation,
playing with a child, writing a report,
    greeting a stranger, doing a favor?
Every act should be done in love?
    Really?

Yes, really.

Sometimes we com-partmentalize our lives. We think this part of our lives (praying, going to church, giving alms) is religious, and this part (folding socks, attending a meeting, greeting a stranger) is not. But love can be the underlying constant in all that we do. Love can make our lives whole.

For reflection

1. What are some of the signs that a certain act is done in love or not?

2. What is your definition of love?

Suggested Scripture

ROMANS 13:8–10
Love is the fulfillment of the law

1 JOHN 4:7–21
God's love and our love

For prayer and play

Keep track today (either mentally or by making a list) of all the acts you do. Are all done in love? Or pretend the segment of John's letter above was written specifically for you. Write John a response to all that he wrote.

12. Every encounter is sacred

Every encounter is sacred,
whether with loved one
  or stranger;
whether brief
  or prolonged,
planned or unexpected,
desired or dreaded.
Every encounter is sacred,
for it can open us up
  to wider possibilities
and impel us toward caring,
thus freeing us
from a pinched life
  of self-preoccupation.

When I was four-teen years old, I met Dr. Thomas Dooley, a former Navy doctor who ministered tire-lessly to the sick in Laos before the Vietnam War. I had read several of his books, so I eagerly went to a talk he gave at a local high school. Afterwards I shook his hand. I know that brief encounter with that great man had a direct impact on my deci-sion (a few years later) to become a nun. Not all encounters are that memorable, of course, but (as the poem says) all encounters are sacred.

For reflection

1. Have you ever had a rather brief encounter with some-one that had a great impact on your life?

2. The poem offers several rea-sons why encounters can be sacred. Can you think of some other reasons?

Suggested Scripture

GENESIS 12:1–9
   The call of Abraham

JEREMIAH 1:4–10
   The call of Jeremiah

For prayer and play

Someone has said, "A person wrapped up in himself or her-self is a very small package." Keep track of all your encoun-ters with others today—the brief, the prolonged; the planned, the unexpected; the desired, the dreaded. What did these encounters call forth from you? Or reflect on the two calls from Scripture listed above. How are they similar? How are they different?

13. Friend, you are home to me

Friend, you are home to me.
Within the walls of your good company,
I come and lay my burdens down.

I take off my coat and sit down.
I slip out of my shoes
and sip the steaming tea
 you have brewed just for me.

You settle down beside me
 and ask, "How are you doing?"
Then you listen to all I have to say.
You ask me questions.
You make no judgments.

Sometimes all you say is "I see,"
and even that comforts me.

Friend, you are home to me.
Within your shelter,
I am more of who I am,
 and more of who I want to be.

In Robert Frost's poem "The Death of the Hired Man," one of the characters says, "Home is the place where, when you have to go there, they take you in." It's a beautiful definition of home and an appropriate image for friendship. For me, friendship has been the greatest blessing of my life. What about you?

For reflection.

1. Have you ever experienced the kind of friendship described in this poem? Have you ever been the "recipient" as well as the "dispenser" of such tenderness and understanding?

2. What do you think the final sentence in this poem is saying?

Suggested Scripture

RUTH
   Ruth and Naomi's friendship

JOHN 15:11-17
   Love and friendship

For prayer and play

Pray for some of your best friends today whether they are living or deceased. Reflect on some of the happy and hard times you shared together. Thank God for them. Or reflect on some of the qualities you feel are essential for friendship. How do you personally measure up against your list?

14. God the Creator is not prim and proper

God the Creator
  is not prim and proper;
  not timid, strait-laced, decorous.

The evidence?
Have you ever
seen a baboon's rainbow-colored butt,
  or heard a fuchsia parrot squawk,
  or smelled a skunk,
  or bit into a jalapeño pepper,
  or gotten some pesky burrs stuck
    all over your pant legs?
The Creator of such an array
is not demure, but rather,
something of a prankster.

Someone has said that the natural world is the "primary scriptures." In other words, just as the Bible reveals who God is, so does all of creation. The English writer Evelyn Underhill wrote, "Every tit-mouse is a celestial messenger, and every thrusting bud is charged with the full significance of life."

For reflection

1. Even as children we used to ask, "What is God like?" Based on the natural world, how would you begin to answer that question?

2. What are some of the other aspects of God's creation (besides baboon butts!) that fascinate or amaze you?

Suggested Scripture

PSALM 33
  God's power and providence

LUKE 13:18–21
  Parables of the mustard seed and yeast

For prayer and play

Draw up a list of qualities you believe God has simply from your observations and interactions with the natural world. Or browse on the Internet or in a book on some aspect of creation—for example, orchids, turtles, hummingbirds, corn, snowflakes, bees, photosynthesis, the sun, etc. Turn your browsing into wonder and praise of God the Creator of all.

15. The greatest sin

The greatest sin
is not lust, greed,
   pride, or murder.
The greatest sin
is to make God
   unattractive.
It is, by the way we live our faith,
to make others say,
"If that's what God is like,
   I'm afraid of him."
Or, "If that's what God is like,
   I want no part of him."
Or, "If that's what God is like,
   ho hum."

Throughout the history of Christianity, some individuals have debated over the relative seriousness of certain sins. Some have argued that the greatest sin is pride or hypocrisy. Others maintain it is the taking of a life or the refusal to forgive. This poem gives a different answer. In doing so, it raises the question: "Who do I say God is by the way I live my faith?"

For reflection

1. What do you think are some of the most serious sins we humans can commit? Why?

2. How attractive do you make God by the way you live your faith?

Suggested Scripture

PSALM 51
Prayer of repentance

LUKE 6:37–42
Judging others

For prayer and play

After reflecting on Psalm 51, compose your own prayer of sorrow and repentance for your sins and failings. Or reflect on some individuals you know (either personally or indirectly through others or history) who make God attractive by the way they live their lives. How do they do it?

16. Grief

[1]

Where you once stood,
  now only emptiness.
Where you were so firmly fixed,
  nothing.
Will it be like this forever?
Or will time
fill the vacuum with something:
  a cluster of small distractions,
  the scraggly grass of routine,
    a wash of loose stones?

I'm new at grieving.
Someone please tell me
What can I expect?
Surely this throbbing ache
  will subside.
Surely this anxiety for tomorrow
  will ease.
Surely something will come
to fill this unbearable void.

[2]

Five months after you died,
I woke up terrified,
   thinking: "Something awful
     is about to happen.
It's something I can't prevent.
It will be irreversible.
It will leave me inconsolable.
It will alter my life forever."

Then it hit me: You were dead.
And I knew what I was dreading
had already taken place:
   You're gone...you're really, really
   gone.

Grief is a mystery. It is unlike anything else we experience. For many, grief comes in waves. We may be feeling fine. Then something happens—we hear a particular song, we visit a place we frequented with our loved one, we see a certain photograph—and grief is triggered. We sense anew our profound loss, and we are enveloped in sorrow all over again.

For reflection

1. What has been your experience of grief? Do any words or phrases in these poems resonate with your experience?

2. When individuals are grieving, what can others do to help or support them?

Suggested Scripture

2 SAMUEL 1:17–27
  David's lament for Saul and Jonathan

JOHN 11:17–44
  Jesus raises Lazarus

For prayer and play

We grieve not only the loss of loved ones but other losses too—such as a job, our youth, a particular place, a pet, our health. Make a list of the loved ones you have lost as well as some of the other significant losses you have experienced in life. Who helped you to deal with these losses? Or, after reflecting on David's elegy for Saul and Jonathan, write your own elegy for one of your losses.

17. Habakkuk the prophet

Habakkuk the prophet
carried food to farmers
   working in the fields.
Nice guy, wouldn't you say?
But legend has it,
an angel swooped down one day
   and picked him up by his hair
and carried him all the way
   to a lion's den,
      where Daniel sat hungry.

Now, I'm wondering:
   what would the angel have done,
      if Habakkuk had been bald?

I needn't worry, though.
For angels can snatch us up
by whatever is handy:
   an arm, an ear, a belt, the collar of a shirt,
      or even a big toe.
Angels in the service of God are,
   if nothing else, resourceful.

While I was caring for my elderly parents, I shared with a priest friend of mine my anxiety for them. Would they fall? Would they have to suffer much? Which one would die first? Would their deaths be quick or prolonged? At one point my friend said to me, "Melannie, remember that God has a personal relationship with each of your parents. And God loves them more than even you do. Maybe you just have to trust more in God's love for each of them and not worry so much." He was absolutely right, of course. Now whenever I find myself worrying or fretting over a friend or family member, I try to trust more in God's love for them, a love that is, "if nothing else, resourceful."

For reflection

1. Do you ever worry and fret about loved ones? What do you do with your worry?

2. Have you ever felt pursued or grabbed by an angel or even by God? If so, describe the experience.

Suggested Scripture

JUDGES 6:11–24
The call of Gideon

LUKE 15:11–32
The parable of the prodigal son

For prayer and play

Read prayerfully the parable of the prodigal son, focusing your attention on the father. What kind of man is he? What are some of the ways he demonstrates love and forgiveness? Do you hope God is like him? Or get a copy of Francis Thompson's poem "The Hound of Heaven." Read it prayerfully (aloud if possible). What does this poem say about God's "pursuing" love?

18. The hawk

I asked the Hawk,
"How can you kill
  that cute little bunny?
How can you seize
his furry body
  with your sharp claws,
rip it apart with your hooked beak,
and devour his
  still warm and wiggling flesh?"

The Hawk replied:
"If you can't understand how,
then you know pitifully little
  about hunger.
Have you never been seized
by a craving so deep
it possessed your whole being—
if not for flesh
then what about for love, meaning,
  or Divinity?"

One day as I was out walking in the park, a hawk swooped down from the sky like an arrow, nailed a sparrow with its talons, and carried it off. It happened so fast, all I had time for was a whispered "Wow!" Of course, I immediately began to feel sorry for the poor sparrow, but at the same time I found myself in awe of the hawk. What stealth, what concentration, what swiftness, what accuracy! Thomas Merton, the Trappist monk, once wrote that the hawk should be studied by saints and mystics. This poem grew out of my hawk experience and Merton's comment.

For reflection

1. What do you know about hunger—not merely for food, but for "love, meaning, or Divinity"?

2. What can saints, mystics, and all of us learn from the hawk?

Suggested Scripture

ISAIAH 40:31
Those who hope in the Lord

JOB 39:26–30
The hawk

For prayer and play

Be a bird watcher today. Observe sparrows, robins, wrens, swallows, hawks, sea gulls, geese—whatever birds happen to be your neighbors. Jot down some of your observations. What did you learn from these birds? Did any questions arise from your bird watching? Or reflect on some of the deepest hungers of your heart. What can you do to satisfy some of these profound cravings? Can it be a good thing that some hungers remain unsatisfied? Why or why not?

19. Heaven is closer than we thought

Cradling a newborn in one's arms,
   succumbing to a great aunt's charms,
laughing around a table with friends,
   being at odds, then making amends.

Hearing the geese honking in their flight,
   comforting a neighbor in her plight,
turning the pages of a good book,
   stopping on the shore for one more look.

Puttering alone among the flowers,
   playing Scrabble for hours and hours,
singing along to a favorite song,
   sensing a loved one near though long gone.

These convince us beyond a doubt:
   heaven is closer than we thought.

For reflection

1. Do any of the examples of ordinary experiences above resonate with your own experience? If so, how?

2. What are some of the other places you seek and find God in your everyday life?

Suggested Scripture

JOHN 2:1-12
  The wedding at Cana

TITUS 2:1—3:8
  Transformation of life

For prayer and play

Read the following quotes prayerfully. What do you think or feel about each one?

- *"Spirituality is meeting God in all that life is."* (Patricia Livingston)

- *"You do not have to be holy to see God in all things. You have only to play as a child with an unselfish heart."* (Matthew Kelty)

- *"Sometimes (our faith) will call us to great, even heroic actions, but mostly it will mean nothing more dramatic than meeting the small, everyday demands and opportunities of our work-a-day world, the perpetual give and take of our ordinary life."* (Evelyn Underhill)

20. He calmed the raging tempest

He calmed the raging tempest
  with but a word or two.
He subdued the winds,
quelled the waves,
  and cut off all the rain.

Little wonder
  the apostles were terrified.
For each one was thinking:
"If he can tame a gale such as this,
  what might he bridle in me?"

When the Holy Spirit came down on that first Pentecost, the disciples were filled with boldness, passion, and vitality. In fact, they were so enthusiastic, some onlookers thought they were drunk. Enthusiasm is a hallmark of Christian discipleship. But there is another side to discipleship that deserves attention: discipline or self-control. This poem calls attention to that essential component of Christian discipleship.

For reflection

1. What kinds of things in the apostles might have needed "bridling"? Is there anything in you that needs bridling?

2. What could the waves, winds, and rain represent in your life?

Suggested Scripture

MARK 4:35–41
The calming of the storm at sea

PHILIPPIANS 2:5–8
Jesus became obedient unto death

For prayer and play

The British writer Caryl Phillips wrote, "It is not how much you want it; it's what you are prepared to give up." Reflect on several things you really wanted in life and were successful at attaining. Next to all of them list what you had to give up in order to obtain each one. Or compose a prayer to Jesus asking him to help you be a better follower of his. Ask him to help you with those things in yourself that still need "bridling."

21. Homesickness

Homesickness is an aching for the past:
   the house we grew up in,
   our mother's apple strudel,
   the companionship of friends now gone,
a simpler age.

The danger:
we can pine so much for what was,
we miss out on what is.
If we take up permanent residence
   in the past,
we forsake life's journey into the future.

But homesickness can also be
an aching for the future:
   a better world here on earth,
   our final home in heaven,
   the reunion with lost loved ones,
   Beatific Visioning.
This kind of homesickness
   is blest gift indeed,
nudging us forward into eternity.

I experienced profound homesickness when I entered the convent at age 17. I missed the house I grew up in, the farm, my family, my friends, even the dog and cats. At times the ache was so severe, I was tempted to leave my new life in the convent and return to the world I knew and loved so much. As I grow older, I find myself experiencing a new kind of homesickness— not for the past, but for the future; not for an earthly home, but for a heavenly one.

For reflection

1. What has been your experience of homesickness for the past? How did you (or are you) dealing with it?

2. Have you ever experienced homesickness for the future? If so, what has that experience been like for you?

Suggested Scripture

PSALM 84
Prayer of the pilgrim

JOHN 16:25–33
Jesus returning to the Father

For prayer and play

Reflect on the word "home" today. What are some of the words or phrases it connotes for you personally? Or write a prayer asking God for the gift of homesickness for the future. Tell God why you especially need this gift at this time in your life.

22. I am a wooer of words

I am a wooer of words.
I hang out in places words frequent:
   like novels, newspapers,
   dictionaries, thesauri.

I have an arsenal of pick-up lines
to befriend them.
I play with them and, at times,
   have been known
to fall shamelessly in love with their sounds
   like *dolorous, hydraulic,* and *hissy fit.*

My aim is always the same:
to get words to do
   what I want them to do.
Sometimes they readily comply—
as the words in this sentence just did.
Other times they have a mind of their own.

They sit stubbornly on the page
with arms folded tightly across their chests
   (whether *flat*, *brawny*, or *voluptuous*)
and refuse *to budge* (or *dislodge*
   from their staid position).
Or they stick on the tip of my tongue
never to see the light of day.
Sometimes words *plod*
   when I want them to *dance*,
they *enervate* when I want them to *thrill*,
they *bellow* when I want them to *susurrate*.
Sometimes words abandon me altogether
and I have to start the whole process
   all over again.

I am a wooer of words.
It is a difficult but delightful
   engagement.

I love words. I love their sounds, their histories, their beauty, their power. As a writer, I naturally hang around words quite a bit. While writing, I often consult a dictionary or thesaurus to find the "perfect" word for the occasion. Sometimes one word leads to another and then another, until I find myself hopelessly lost in the pages. As the poem implies, words have a charm and a mind of their own. For me, engaging with them on a daily basis is a very pleasurable occupation.

For reflection

1. Why is the image of a "wooer of words" appropriate for a poet?

2. To what extent do you engage with words? What has that experience been like for you?

Suggested Scripture

PROVERBS 15:23; 25:11
Power of words

JOHN 6:60–69
Words of eternal life

For prayer and play

Pull out a dictionary or thesaurus and begin to read it slowly and prayerfully. What did you learn about specific words from doing this? Or try to learn one new word each day this week. Thank God for the magic and mystery of words.

23. I cannot take your pain away *(to Margaret)*

I cannot take your pain away.
I cannot give you back your youth,
restore your health,
  or make your mind clear and sharp again.
I cannot fill the hollow of your loneliness.
I cannot say, "I know exactly how you feel,"
  or "Everything's going to be okay."

But I can sit with you.

I can hold your hand if you want me to.
I can be silent or recite the words
we are both straining now to live:
  "Yea, though I walk through the valley
    of the shadow of death,
  I will fear no evil: for Thou art with me."
I cannot do your believing for you,
but I can and will continue to love you
  forever.

Watching a loved one suffer is perhaps the greatest cross we can bear—especially when we are powerless to relieve that suffering. At times like these, we resort to simple human touch, presence, and prayer. And all the while we continue to love.

For reflection

1. Have you ever watched a loved one suffer and been powerless to relieve their suffering? If so, what did you do?

2. Who helped you when you were suffering? What did they do?

Suggested Scripture

PSALM 121
 My help comes from God

LUKE 22:39–46
 The agony in the garden

For prayer and play

Visit a friend or family member who is homebound or in a nursing home. Offer them the gift of your loving companionship. Or write a thank you to someone who helped you when you were suffering or in need. Even if the incident happened many years ago, a thank you is still appropriate.

24. Jesus, you cleansed the Temple

Jesus, you cleansed the Temple in Jerusalem.
You turned tables over,
  set doves and lambs free,
    and chased out all the money changers,
while yelling, "My house shall be
  a house of prayer—not a den of thieves!"

Jesus, come now and do the same in me.
For I too have set up clutter
  where sacred space was meant to be.
I too am caging living things
  with my excessive need to control.
I too am enamored
  by profit, glitz, and material gain.

Come, Jesus, reclaim me as your own.
Come cleanse the temple of me.

Some paintings of Jesus are too "mousey" for my taste. They depict a Jesus who is weak and wimpy. What a contrast to the Jesus who cleansed the Temple. All four gospels record this strange event with vivid details: he made a whip out of cords, he spilled the coins of the money changers, he overturned tables and chairs, he drove out the money changers and the dove sellers, and he barred anyone from carrying anything through the temple area. What a display of power, indignation, courage, and conviction!

For reflection

1. Why do you think Jesus cleansed the Temple in this way? (Perhaps a commentary on this passage or the footnotes in your Bible might help here.)

2. What is some of the "clutter" you'd like Jesus to clear out? Are you "caging" any "living things" by your "need to control"?

Suggested Scripture

MATTHEW 21:12–13;
MARK 11:15–19;
LUKE 19:45–48;
JOHN 2:13–21
  Cleansing of the Temple

For prayer and play

Read all four accounts of the cleansing of the Temple. Reflect on how they are alike and how they are different. Or compose a prayer to Jesus, the One who cleanses.

25. Jonah

It wasn't bad
   as places go,
  this belly of the whale.
Better down here
   than any up there,
  safer calm than gale.

Or so he thought
   until the space
  twixt refusals and assents
became a nowhere
   driving him to beg
  deliverance.

I have this image of Jonah sitting in the darkness of the belly of the whale, his knees drawn up to his chin. He's mad at God. He's mad at the world. He does *not* want to go and preach to those awful Ninevites, because they just might repent—and then God would forgive them. (He knows the vast extent of God's love and mercy.) So Jonah ran away. But God was persistent. He found Jonah hiding in the boat and caused a mighty storm. Jonah was persistent too. He was even willing to drown in the churning sea rather than say yes to God. But God foiled Job's plans. God sent this whale that swallowed Job whole. Now what? Job sat and sat. Was it his imagination or were the walls of this belly closing in upon him? After only a short time, Job cried out, "OK, God, you win. I'll go."

For reflection

1. In the poem, Jonah first thinks, "Safer calm than gale." Is calm always safer than gale? When have you experienced "a gale" that turned out to be a blessing? Can too much calm be dangerous?

2. Have you ever said "no" or "not yet" to God? What happened?

Suggested Scripture

JONAH

MARK 14:32–42
The agony in the garden

For prayer and play

Jonah's story is quite extraordinary. Pretend you are a talk show host and have Jonah as a guest on your show. What questions would you ask? What answers might Jonah give? Or prayerfully reflect on the agony in the garden. You might want to read it in a garden if possible. Pretend you are there with Jesus. What would you say to him? What would you do?

26. The Magi

They wore silks and taffeta,
rode gangly camels, bore precious gifts:
  gold, incense, and myrrh.

They followed that certain star
over mountain tops, down into valleys,
  across barren plains.

They sought bearings from
passing caravans, strangers in cities
  and even a king.

Then, upon arrival, they found
no transcendent deity, no dazzling
  theophany, no blinding epiphany,
just a little boy on his mother's knee.

In his book *The Holy Longing*, Father Ronald Rolheiser writes, "The central mystery within all of Christianity, undergirding everything else, is the mystery of the incarnation." This poem celebrates that mystery. The Magi have always fascinated me with their peculiar attire, their erudite learning, their arduous trek. But I wonder, how did they feel when they came upon the little boy Jesus and his humble, young parents? What were their thoughts? What did they say? What did they talk about on the way home? We can only imagine.

For reflection

1. Do you agree with Father Rolheiser's statement about the incarnation? Why or why not?

2. How do you think the Magi felt when they finally found Jesus with his parents?

Suggested Scripture

MATTHEW 2:1–12
The visit of the Magi

LUKE 24:13–35
The disciples on the road to Emmaus

For prayer and play

Write a dialogue which answers that question, "What did the Magi talk about on their way home?" Or read Henry van Dyke's classic *The Other Wise Man*, or watch the DVD adaptation, *The Fourth Wise Man*.

27. Make up your mind

Make up your mind once and for all.
Do you believe in the
   ultimate goodness of life,
      or not?
Do you stake your claim on the final
   victory of love over hate,
      or not?
Do you trust in a Higher Power, or not?

Why do you keep vacillating?
Is consistency that impossible for you?

Look at it this way:
Little good can come from living out
   of a maybe.
A definitive yes would strengthen
   who you are and all you do.
It would channel your energies
and propel you forward
   in a more meaningful direction.

Come on now. It's either yes or no.
Say yes already. Say yes.

This poem is about commitment. Commitment is deeply rooted in our basic convictions about life. If we believe *this*, then we will make *these* kinds of choices. If we believe *that*, then *that* is the kind of person we will become. Commitment carries us to places we otherwise would have avoided. Once there, commitment keeps us standing there no matter how tempted we may be to run away.

For reflection

1. How do you personally answer the first three questions posed at the beginning of this poem?

2. Are you happy with the person you are becoming by your commitments? Why or why not?

Suggested Scripture

MARK 10:17–31
The rich young man

EPHESIANS 4:25–32
Christian conduct

For prayer and play

Reflect on your commitments today. What do you really believe about life, faith, love? How are your commitments influencing your choices? What kind of a person are you becoming because of your commitments? Or read prayerfully the story of the rich young man and reflect on these questions: What is Jesus' attitude toward this man? What do *you* think of him? What prevents him from following Jesus? What do you think about Jesus' words on wealth and riches? What implications do they have for you personally?

28. Matthew

When Matthew got up
   from his customs table,
he left behind
   tall stacks of coins.
I wonder,
whatever happened to them?
I picture a mad scuffle
   with pushing and shoving,
   yelling and cursing,
and a table
picked clean like a carcass
   by vultures.

I envy Matthew's freedom
to walk away from it all—
until I recall,
he wasn't walking *away* from *something*,
he was walking *toward Someone*.

I have seen several paintings of the call of Matthew. They usually emphasize the power of Jesus' call as well as Matthew's total response to that call. But I have yet to see a painting that depicts what happened when Matthew walked away from all his money.

For reflection

1. What's the difference between walking *away* and walking *toward*?

2. What factors do you think enabled Matthew to leave all for Jesus?

Suggested Scripture

MATTHEW 9:9; LUKE 5:27–32
   The call of Matthew

MARK 1:16–20
   The call of the first disciples

For prayer and play

Prayerfully read the two accounts of the call of Matthew (Levi). What strikes you about the two accounts? Or reflect on a time when you felt called by Jesus to do something. What was your response? What factors contributed to your response?

29. Mr. Spider

Mr. Spider, I see your web
hanging from the porch railing.
It's probably been there for weeks,
but I just noticed it today,
for the morning dew
   has given it away.
Tiny white beads of moisture
glisten on every delicate strand,
calling my attention
   to your web's exquisite design.
Until the dew evaporates,
be prepared to go hungry,
for no critter is apt
   to be entangled in your trap.

But then again, I'm a critter,
and I've been sitting here
   for quite some time, rapt in wonder
at your amazing artistry.

Mr. Spider, I say with certainty,
   your web has snared me!

The French writer Simone Weil wrote, "We do not obtain the most precious gifts by going in search of them, but by waiting for them." She felt the basis of authentic prayer was simply the ability to pay attention.

For reflection

1. Have you ever been "snared" by some beautiful or intriguing aspect of creation as was the speaker in this poem? If so, what? If not, why not?

2. Do you agree with Simone Weil above or not? Why?

Suggested Scripture

PSALM 131
Humble trust in God

MATTHEW 17:1–8
The Transfiguration

For prayer and play

Pay attention to what you pay attention to for one day. What did you learn about yourself from this experiment? Or pay attention to the quotations below:

- *"The moment one gives close attention to anything, even a blade of grass, it becomes a mysterious, awesome, indescribably magnificent world in itself."* (Henry Miller)

- *"Tell me to what you pay attention and I will tell you who you are."* (Jose Ortega y Gasset)

- *"Attention is an act of love, an act of connection."* (Julia Cameron)

30. My mother's yellow jacket

When my mother died
and we divvied up
   her few belongings,
I took her yellow jacket.
Now on days when I'm missing her
   or feeling lonesome
   or misunderstood,
I reach for that jacket.
I slip my arms into the sleeves,
   pull the zipper up,
   plop the hood over my head
   and put my hands
      into the two deep pockets.
Then I close my eyes
and just stand there
   for a minute or two,
swathed and comforted
by a mother's enduring love.

Years ago a sister was being installed as president of a college. The local bishop presided at the Mass of Installation. Right before the final blessing, he paused and asked the sister to stand up. Then he invited her parents to stand up too. Then the bishop said, "Sister, when things get rough—and they will—remember the unconditional love of your mother and father." When we experience difficult times, hopefully we have someone in our life who loves us unconditionally—just as God does.

For reflection

1. Do you have any keepsakes from someone you love?

2. Who loves you unconditionally? Whom do you love unconditionally?

Suggested Scripture

SONG OF SONGS 8:6b–7
True love

JOHN 19:25–27
Jesus and his mother

For prayer and play

Reflect on a keepsake. Who is it from? How long have you had it? Why do you keep it? Or reflect on someone who loves you unconditionally. How do they demonstrate their unconditional love for you?

31. No matter what

No matter how far you have strayed,
   God will find you.
No matter how deep your anguish,
   God will comfort you.
No matter how serious your illness,
   God will heal you.
No matter how grave your sin,
   God will forgive you.
No matter how low you have fallen,
   God will raise you up.
No matter how weak you are,
   God will give you strength.
No matter how stubborn your will,
   God will urge you forward.
No matter how cold your heart,
   God will warm you.
No matter what,
   God will keep on loving you.

Regina Brett, a columnist for *The Cleveland Plain Dealer*, wrote, "God loves you because of who God is, not because of anything you did or didn't do." It's humbling to realize we do not earn God's love. We choose to do loving things not to win God's favor. Rather, we do loving things because we know God loves us— and we know how good that love feels! Every time we love we are passing on part of the love we have already received from God and from others.

For reflection

1. Do any of the words or phrases in this poem resonate with your personal experience?

2. Has your loving ever reflected God's love described in this poem? If so, when and how?

Suggested Scripture

2 SAMUEL 11:1—12:25
The sin and repentance of David

ISAIAH 49:14–16
God will never forget you

For prayer and play

Reflect on individuals in your life who have reflected God's love for you: family members, friends, teachers, coaches, colleagues, priests, nuns, neighbors. Be specific: what kinds of love did they show you: comforting? forgiving? strengthening? healing? lifting? urging? stretching? Or read prayerfully the story of David's sin and repentance. What factors made David's sin so terrible? How does Nathan demonstrate great courage? How does David demonstrate sincere sorrow for what he did?

32. The obituary

In the end, most of us get
a three-inch column of type listing
   our parents, spouse,
   children, brothers, and sisters.
It tells where we lived
and what we did for a living;
   the degrees we earned and
   awards we won;
and a personal achievement:
   he was an usher at St. Procop's;
   she crocheted quilts for Birthright;
   he collected beer cans;
   she groomed dogs.
An entire life is squeezed
   into twenty lines of print.
Fortunately the obituary
   heaven writes for each of us
is longer than the *Summa Theologica*.
It notes every prayer uttered in faith,
   every pain borne in hope,
     every deed done in love.

I often read the obituaries in the daily newspaper. I sometimes think how unfair it is to squeeze an entire life into a few inches of print. I'm confident, though, that God knows and cherishes everything about us—our every ache, joy, struggle, and achievement.

For reflection

1. Do you ever read the obituaries? Why or why not?

2. Do you think God "notes" our prayer, pain, and deeds? Explain your answer.

Suggested Scripture

WISDOM 3:1–6
The souls of the just

LUKE 12:16–21
Parable of the rich fool

For prayer and play

Read the obituaries prayerfully today. What did you learn? How did it make you feel? Or write your own obituary. This need not be depressing at all. What do you want to be remembered for?

33. Perfectionism

Perfectionism is a cruel taskmaster.
Scant is her reward for your
  onerous labors.
She bestows no peace, no joy,
  no closure.
She never says, "Well done!
  Good job! Take a rest!"

Instead all she ever says is
  "More! More! More!"
Even if you meet her demands
in a given area of your life,
she quickly finds fault
with all the rest of you
  and persists in her relentless nagging.

Why strain yourself
for her unwinnable approval?
Far better to expend yourself
on befriending one of these:
Humility, Patience, Loose Ends.

Perfectionism is the disposition that says anything short of perfect is unacceptable. Although it is an impossible standard to live by, many of us get caught up in it. But why do we? As the poem suggests, Perfectionism "bestows no peace, no joy, no closure." And "scant is her reward for your onerous labors." The poem offers some antidotes for perfectionism in the last line: humility, patience, and the ability to live with loose ends.

For reflection

1. Do you ever get caught up in the pursuit of perfectionism? If so, what impels you? If not, why not?

2. The poem suggests befriending Humility, Patience, and Loose Ends. Which of these (if any) have you already befriended? Which (if any) do you feel you could befriend more?

Suggested Scripture

LUKE 6:27–36
   Love of enemies

PSALM 25
   *Prayer for forgiveness and
   guidance*

For prayer and play

This poem personifies Perfectionism. Write a paragraph or poem that personifies one of these: Humility, Patience, or Loose Ends. Or, after reflecting on Jesus' words about love of enemies, write a paragraph or poem on Mercy. Or cite evidence from the gospels that shows Jesus' befriending of humility, patience, and loose ends.

34. Poison ivy

Poison Ivy, do you ever regret your toxicity—
how just one ounce of your noxious oil
could infect over 20,000 people?
And how a trace of your oil
   left on our clothing
can still contaminate five years later?

Do you ever wish
   you were more approachable—
like your cousin Aloe Vera,
   whose transparent inner sap
      promotes soothing and healing?

Even a slight brush against any part of you—
   leaf, stem, berry, root—
provokes irritation, inflammation,
   and aggravating itch.
Don't you see how your quest
   for self-preservation has gone askew,
causing all of us now to steer clear of you?

Poison Ivy, you remind me
   of some people I know.

Self-preservation is a strong drive in all living things. Squirrels scamper up trees, geese hiss and flap their wings, dogs growl, birds quickly take flight, and poison ivy exudes a toxic oil—all in an effort to preserve themselves from danger or death. We humans too learn techniques to preserve ourselves from perceived dangers. Some of these techniques are good and praiseworthy, for they prevent us from being treated poorly or unjustly by others. But sometimes our self-preservation instinct can go "askew" and we end up becoming totally unapproachable.

For reflection

1. What are some of the techniques you employ to preserve your rights and dignity as a human being?

2. How approachable are you? Why does it matter?

Suggested Scripture

MATTHEW 4:23–25
 The approachability of Jesus

ROMANS 15:1–6
 Patience and self-denial

For prayer and play

Skim one of the gospels and list the various individuals or groups that came to Jesus because he was so approachable. Or list the qualities you believe make individuals approachable. How do you measure up to your list?

35. President Lincoln

He was six feet four, and lean,
with large hands that said,
  "I know how to wield an axe."
When out and about
he wore a long black coat
  and a stovepipe hat,
which made him seem even taller.
As president,
he bore the weight of personal tragedy
  and the entire Civil War.
And in the end he freed the slaves
and preserved the Union.

Had Lincoln been
  only five feet three,
he would have been
a man of great height.
For stature such as his is measured
  not in inches,
    but in righteousness.

Recently I visited Lincoln's Cottage at the Soldiers' Home in Washington, D.C. This is where Lincoln and his family resided from June to November in 1862, 1863, and 1864. Often Lincoln mounted his horse and rode to the White House to work, a journey of just a few miles. Amazingly, he sometimes rode alone. One time someone shot a hole in his stovepipe hat. The visit to this historic house impressed me very much. Long an admirer of Lincoln, I was given even more reasons to esteem this man. The tour of Lincoln's Cottage also inspired this poem.

For reflection

1. What are your thoughts and views of President Lincoln?

2. Reflect on a few of your heroes today. Why do you admire these individuals?

Suggested Scripture

PSALM 1
Persons of integrity

COLOSSIANS 1:15–29
Preeminence of Christ

For prayer and play

Our society holds up many different kinds of heroes: athletes, political leaders, scientists, entertainers, religious individuals, business leaders, humanitarians. Write a short reflection on how Jesus is the real hero our world needs today. Or make a list of some of your heroes. What does your list reveal about you and your values?

36. The river

Another life runs through us
like a mighty underground river.
It is always there
   though never quite seen,
lapping incessantly
   on the dry ground of our being,
exerting a powerful sway
   on all we do.

In its gushing current
angels bob and play,
   as do our beloved dead.
Into these same waters
I dip my pen from time to time
and snare an image, a story,
   a poem.

In her wonderful book *The Sound of Paper*, Julia Cameron says that inspiration is like a stream that artists tap into. "Our creativity is a spiritual gift with its taproot in the Spirit and not in our own will." Through the ages, she writes, great artists have insisted they were merely channels for divine energy. She concludes, "I like knowing that there is something larger than myself, larger than all of us, that moves into the world when we are accessible to it as a conduit."

For reflection

1. What do you think of Julia Cameron's thoughts on inspiration and creativity?

2. Have you ever experienced the "mighty underground river" or "the stream" as described here? If so, reflect on that experience.

Suggested Scripture

JUDITH 16:13–16
Judith's canticle

LUKE 1:46–55
Mary's canticle

For prayer and play

Read prayerfully the canticles by Judith and by Mary. Do you detect some similarities? some differences? If you feel moved, compose your own canticle of praise to God. Or get in touch with the river or stream of divine energy today by composing your own piece of art work, by reading a favorite piece of literature, or by listening to a favorite piece of music.

37. The road to God

The road to God
  is not long.
You need not cross the sea
  to find Divinity.
You need not trek across vast plains
  or barren deserts,
nor hack through dense jungles.
You need not scale jagged mountains
jutting into the skies.

No, you have only to pause
  and be still.
Then take that single step
  into the deep center
    of who you are.

In one of his sermons, St. Bernard says if you want to meet God, "Enter into your own soul and you will find him." Sometimes we make prayer too complicated, too strenuous. Sometimes we forget that God is nearer to us than we are even to ourselves.

For reflection

1. Reflect on your prayer today. Does it ever get too complicated or strenuous?

2. What is the "single step" you might take today to enter "the deep center / of who you are"?

Suggested Scripture

1 KINGS 19:9–16
Elijah and the still, small voice

PSALM 46:10
Be still and know that I am God

For prayer and play

Just sit with Psalm 46:10 and let it be your mantra today. Or try praying in a new way today.

38. The shortstop

Live your life like a good shortstop.
Dare to stand in the between spaces
  of life's active infield.
Plant yourself firmly yet lightly
  on the balls of your feet.
Crouch forward slightly,
ready to spring in any direction:
  left, right, forward, back.
Build arm strength, work on your range.
Master these essential skills:
  take an angle on the ball, get in front of it,
  block it with your chest if need be.
A temporary bruise is a small price to pay
for preventing the opposition from scoring.

Embrace the fact that more balls
  are hit to you than to any other position.
At every moment in the game you might get
  a sharp grounder, a crazy bouncer,
  a stinging line drive, a popup a mile high—
all off Fortune's bat.

Be poised to glove whatever comes your way
  and humbly make the play.

The game of baseball has often been used as a metaphor for life. Baseball involves making "sacrifice" plays, being thrown a lot of curve balls, and getting home safely as the ultimate goal. To me a double play is as beautiful as a well-coordinated dance move. A diving catch in the outfield blends perfect timing with total commitment. A home run into the upper deck is the marriage of superior hand-eye coordination with brute power. Little wonder many of us enjoy the game so much.

For reflection

1. What might the following represent in real life: "the between spaces," "life's active infield," "work your range," "take an angle on the ball," "Fortune's bat," "glove whatever comes your way"?

2. As a Christian, who or what is "the opposition"? What "temporary bruises" have you experienced in your role as a disciple of Jesus?

Suggested Scripture

MATTHEW 5:13–16
Metaphors of salt and light

JOHN 15:1–8
The vine and the branches

For prayer and play

Jesus is a master of metaphor. After reflecting on his metaphors of salt, light, vine, and branches, choose one that really speaks to you and sit with it for a while and see what happens. Or can you come up with any other metaphors for life or Christian discipleship? If so, compose a prayer or reflection about it.

39. Singing all the way home in the dark

As a little girl I sometimes played
  too long at Beverly's house.
That meant I had to walk home
  in the dark.

I would start out nonchalantly
until I heard a twig snap,
  a swish in the tall grass,
  or the stomp-stomp-stomp
    of an unseen and hungry monster.
Then I would walk a little faster,
then faster and faster until
I broke into a wild run, down the dirt road,
  through the bushes,
  across our front lawn,
  up the steps, and onto our front porch
where I would collapse in a heap,
  gasping for breath, but safe.

But one time I decided
not to run, but to sing:

Row, Row, Row Your Boat,
I've Been Working on the Railroad,
Mary Had a Little Lamb.
The songs steadied my pace.
They gave me courage.
They kept all monsters at bay.
Singing tricked even me
into thinking I was strong and brave.

Today, I'm an adult
still on my way home.
It's late at night and dark at times.
Monsters are hiding all around,
   ready to pounce on me.
And the fear I knew as a child
   rises up in my throat.
That's when I recall
my little trick from childhood,
and I start to sing—
   only this time it's Silent Night,
   Amazing Grace,
   How Great Thou Art.
I plan to keep on singing
all the way home in the dark.

Music is universal, occurring in all cultures. Archeologists have found flutes made of bone that date back nearly 40,000 years. Neuroscientists now tell us that music activates more of the brain than any other stimulus we know. It exerts its strongest effect in the brain's emotional core—especially that area associated with pleasure. Scientists are currently exploring ways music might be used to treat depression, anxiety, and post-traumatic stress disorder. The poet here, as a little girl, knows instinctively the emotional benefits of music. The adult knows too.

For reflection

1. Can you identify with the little girl in this poem? Can you identify with the adult in this poem?

2. What role does music play in your emotional health?

Suggested Scripture

PSALM 98
Sing a new song

REVELATION 1:17–18
Do not be afraid

For prayer and play

Listen to some music today, paying attention to the emotions that are aroused with each piece. Or put some music on and grab some paper and markers. Let yourself get lost in the music, and then draw whatever the music inspires.

40. The skunk

Dear God,
may I suggest:
you didn't have to make
the skunk stink so much?
Instead,
you could have made him
smell like cinnamon,
  gardenias,
  sandalwood,
  lilies-of-the-valley,
or some other fragrance
  you hadn't even invented yet.
One whiff of a scent so sweet
would subdue and enchant
the most aggressive predator.

I humbly submit:
beauty disarms
more effectively
than stench.

Underlying this rather whimsical poem is a serious theme: the need for beauty in everyday life. In her book *A Natural History of the Senses*, Diane Ackerman tells of a friend who insisted Ackerman was paying far too much for her apartment—an apartment that overlooked the park's changing seasons, had a window that captured the sunset every night, and was situated in a charming ethnically diverse neighborhood. When the friend left, Ackerman "watched the sunset's pinwheels of apricot and mauve slowly explode into red ribbons." She knew the beauty that her apartment afforded her every single day was well worth the extra money she paid for rent.

For reflection

1. Take an inventory of the beauty in your life right now. Do you have sufficient beauty? If not, what can you do about it?

2. British writer D. H. Lawrence said, "The human soul needs beauty even more than it needs bread." Do you agree or disagree? Why?

Suggested Scripture

EXODUS 3:4–14
Moses and the burning bush

MATTHEW 6:25–34
Consider the lilies

For prayer and play

Reflect on these quotations about beauty. Then add your own.

- *"The world will be saved by beauty."* (Fedor Dostoevsky)

- *"When beauty overwhelms us, we are close to worship."* (Richard C. Cabot)

- *"Beauty is not caused. It is."* (Emily Dickinson)

- *"Beauty puts a face on God."* (Margaret Brownley)

- *"Let the beauty we love be what we do."* (Rumi)

41. The snake

When God asked Adam
if he had eaten from the Tree,
Adam said yes
  but then blamed Eve.
Eve in turn blamed the snake.
The snake in turn blamed
  his abusive father,
  his neglectful mother,
  his deviant friends,
  his deprived neighborhood,
  the lousy serpentine
    educational system,
  the steady bombardment of
  materialistic values,
and (most of all) his genetic
  predisposition
    to trickery.

Yes, there are factors that mitigate guilt. Yes, there are situations that impinge upon our freedom to choose what is right. At the same time, we humans (like the snake in the poem) are ingenious at fabricating excuses for our boorish and even sinful behavior. Personal responsibility is an endangered species.

For reflection

1. What excuses do you come up with for your less than Christ-like behavior?

2. What does the phrase "accepting personal responsibility for" mean to you?

Suggested Scripture

GENESIS 3
 The Fall

MARK 2:1–12
 The cure of the paralytic

For prayer and play

Rewrite the story of the Fall in contemporary terms and language. Have fun with it! Or read prayerfully the story of the cure of the paralytic. What does this story tell you about friendship? about compassion? about sin? about forgiveness?

42. Space

The distance between heavenly bodies
   is mind boggling:
Our sun—93 million miles from earth;
Proxima Centuri, our next nearest star
   —five light years away from us.
Traveling at the current speed of our rockets,
the journey there would last 100,000 years!
And our galaxy, the Milky Way?
It is 100,000 light years across!
And the Sombrero Galaxy?
It is 28 million light years away from us!

The space in so-called "solid" things
   is just as astounding.
If a proton in an atom were 4 inches long,
   its orbiting electrons would be 4 miles away!
One molecule of iron is
   over 99.999 percent empty space!

What can we deduce from all of this?
The Creator has a fondness
   for elbowroom.

Long before the Bible was written, long before Jesus walked our earth, God spoke to us through creation. Even today the natural world remains a major revelation of God. The more I learn about stars, snowflakes, oceans, tulips, otters, and the molecular structure of iron, the more I find myself saying, "Wow! What must God be like?"

For reflection

1. What do you think and feel about the scientific facts presented in this poem?

2. What are some of the deductions you have made about God based on your experience of the natural world?

Suggested Scripture

PSALM 65
   Thanksgiving for God's blessings

1 JOHN 1:1–4
   The Word of Life

For prayer and play

Get lost in a science book or website today. Or go outside tonight and stand under the stars. Or reflect on the role space plays in your life. What effect do open spaces have on you? What about tight places?

43. Thank you, God

Thank you, God, for:
apples,
bluebirds, cinnamon,
diversity, eggs, friendship,
generosity, healing,
ice cream, jokes,
kisses, learning, music,
neurons, oceans, popcorn,
questions, rain,
stars, technology,
unicorns, valentines,
warmth, x-rays, yearnings,
and zippers.

This poem uses the alphabet as its foundation. It thanks God for specific things—from the tiny to the huge, from the important to the seemingly trivial. You might question some of my choices. Why "popcorn" when I could have chosen "prayer"? Why "cinnamon" when I could have chosen "Christmas"? All I can say is this is one version of the poem. I have written countless others. Other days I have thanked God for cats, dogs, family, orchids, tenderness, Velcro, watermelons, zinc…

For reflection

1. Are there things listed in this poem that you also thank God for? If so, which ones and why?

2. What things are you grateful for that are not listed in this poem? Why are you grateful for them?

Suggested Scripture

PSALM 136
  Hymn of Thanksgiving

LUKE 17:11–19
  Cure of the ten lepers

For prayer and play

On a sheet of paper, write the alphabet down the left side of the page. For each letter list something for which you are especially grateful. You can vary this exercise by choosing specific categories such as flowers, animals, foods, songs, people you know, etc. Or make a conscious effort today to thank people for their great and small services.

44. This is your task in life

This is your task in life:
first, befriend yourself.
Learn to enjoy being with you.

This is task number two:
find good companions
who share your deepest longings,
and are both cheerleader
and goad for you.

And your third task?
Find people in need
and pour upon them
the contents of your heart.

What is the purpose of life? What brings happiness? This poem gives one answer to those questions. Over the years I have collected many other answers from a wide range of people. Here are a few of them:

- *"Know thyself."* (Socrates)

- *"One ought, every day at least, to hear a little song, read a good poem, see a fine picture."* (Goethe)

- *"Do what you can, with what you have, where you are."* (Theodore Roosevelt)

- *"See everything. Overlook a great deal. Improve a little."* (Pope John XXIII)

- *"Find something you like to do. Learn to do it well, and do it in the service of the people."* (Karlene Faith)

For reflection

1. To what extent do you agree or disagree with the advice given in this poem?

2. What do you think it means that our "good companions" are both "cheerleader" and "goad"? Do you have any such people in your life?

Suggested Scripture

MICAH 6:8
   What God requires of you

MATTHEW 5:1–12
   The Beatitudes

For prayer and play

Write your own personal answer to the question: what brings happiness in life? Or go online or search a book of quotations for more advice on happiness and living.

45. The to-do list

Things on our to-do list:
return library books,
  buy birthday card,
pick up eggs and milk,
  cash check,
make dental appointment,
  mop kitchen floor,
stop at dry cleaners,
  get oil change,
return that phone call,
  write that report.

Things that should be on our to-do list:
become a kinder person,
  trust God more,
pray everyday,
  forgive that offense,
say you're sorry,
  reach out to someone in need,
spend time with loved ones,
  enjoy God's creation,
grow up.

Like many people, I have a to-do list on my desk. Every time I accomplish something on my list, I cross it off. I feel good when I do this. In fact, if I do an errand that is not on my to-do list, I quickly write it on my list and then immediately cross it off! (I know I'm not the only person who does this!) But one day, as I was crossing something off my to-do list, the idea for this poem came to me. It raises the question: Are we so preoccupied with our daily small tasks that we lose sight of the more important "tasks" we are called to do as Christians?

For reflection

1. What is on your to-do list? (Your list can be written down or in your head.)

2. What "tasks" are you being called to do as a Christian?

Suggested Scripture

PSALM 27
Trust in God

MATTHEW 22:34–40
The greatest commandment

For prayer and play

Keep a to-do list this week of your ordinary tasks. Can you see how any of these tasks are actually related to the two greatest commandments given by Jesus in Matthew 22? Or compose a to-do list of some of your deepest dreams and longings. Take your list to prayer.

46. Two days before he died

Two days before he died,
  my father stopped reading the newspaper.
Now this was a man who never in his life
  had left the paper unread.

Yet when I walked into the house
that morning, there he was,
  sitting mutely at the kitchen table,
  hands loosely clasped across his stomach,
  eyes fixed on something only he could see
    outside the window past the willow tree.

And there was the newspaper,
folded neatly before him
  where my mother had laid it
    two hours before.

That's when I knew
  Dad would be leaving us soon.
He had no more need of earthly news.

As death neared for my father, he spoke less and stared out the window more. I think he was already dying—in stages—and he knew it. The way I figure it, when one has gotten glimpses of the heavenly kingdom one is about to enter, most of the news in our newspapers must seem pretty trivial.

For reflection

1. Have you received some "glimpses of heaven"? In other words, are there people and events in your life that hint at what heaven must be like?

2. Do you read or view the news everyday? Why or why not?

Suggested Scripture

MARK 13:32–37
   Need for watchfulness

ROMANS 5:1–11
   Faith, hope, and love

For prayer and play

Take a newspaper to prayer today. Note the stories you feel are really important and pray for the people and issues involved. Or reflect on Jesus' words about watchfulness. On a scale of 1 to 10 (10 being the highest) how alert and watchful are you to the things that really matter in life? Give examples. How might you heed Jesus' words more?

47. Uncle Joe

On our drive to his doctor's office,
Uncle Joe reads the signs
   we pass along the way.
He starts out slowly:
   "Gas. Fresh Donuts.
     No parking anytime."
Then more quickly,
   "Stop. Help wanted.
     Copies made.
   Walk-ins welcome.
   No turn on red."

During election time,
he reads the name on every placard
   on every lawn:
   "O'Neal, O'Neal, Watkins,
   O'Neal, Zindrowski, Watkins,
   O'Neal, O'Neal, Watkins,
   Zindrowski, O'Neal, O'Neal,"
and growing weary, says,
   "I think O'Neal's gonna get it."

Reading is one thing
Uncle Joe still remembers how to do.
Long ago he forgot how to shave,
   get dressed and eat unassisted.
A bachelor, he's confused
   about family and friends.
To him I'm just some "nice lady"
   who helps him out every now and then.
He has no idea what year it is,
   where he lives now,
   or that he worked in the steel mill
      for forty years.
But Uncle Joe can still read.
And so he does.
Anything and everything.

Reading, I think,
is the only way
he has left to say,
   "I'm somebody too."

When a friend told me a similar story about her uncle, I was deeply moved. Dementia and Alzheimer's are terrible afflictions. The loss of memory is an awful cross to bear not only for the victim but also for the victim's loved ones. This poem raises the question: In what does our dignity as human beings lie?

For reflection

1. What has been your experience with dementia and/or Alzheimer's? How did this experience make you feel?

2. The poem hints at the tender care of Uncle Joe's niece. When have the needs of others called forth love and tenderness from you?

Suggested Scripture

PSALM 77
  Remembering God's deeds

LUKE 9:23–27
  Conditions of discipleship

For prayer and play

Reach out to someone who is struggling with loss of memory. Or reach out to someone who is dealing with a loved one who has dementia or Alzheimer's. Write a note, make a phone call, pay a visit, pray for him or her, do a small favor.

48. Upon reading *Moby Dick*

Sometimes a big white whale
is a symbol of all the evil
  in the universe.
Sometimes it represents fate
  or all that is beyond human control.
Sometimes a big white whale
stands for an unknowable God,
  or the tragic consequences
    of exploiting the earth's resources.

But sometimes a big white whale
  is just a big white whale.
In our unending quest
to make sense of the cosmos,
we can turn everything
  into a symbol,
forgetting it is best at times
to let a whale be a whale,
  the sun, the sun, a tulip, a tulip,
    a stone, a stone.

> I think this poem is about appreciating things simply for what they are and not for what they do or mean or represent. Amen.

For reflection

1. How good are you at letting things (or people) just be and appreciating their being?

2. Symbolism has its worth, of course. What are some symbols in your life that really speak to you?

Suggested Scripture

PSALM 104:24–30
   Praise God's creation

PHILIPPIANS 4:4–9
   Joy and peace

For prayer and play

Practice appreciating people for who they are today. On a piece of paper, jot down the names of some of the significant people in your life right now. After their names, write down some of the positive characteristics you appreciate in each of them. Or make a mental list of some of the symbols you notice today: a flag, a ring, a company logo, etc. What are some of the great symbols of our Christian faith?

49. We are all breakable

We are all breakable.
The four-day-old infant,
the octogenarian,
the 300-pound sumo wrestler,
the 98-pound gymnast,
the priest, the rabbi, the imam,
the mayor and the governor,
the physics professor,
   the woman who cleans his classroom,
the third-grader with freckles,
the stylist and the letter carrier,
the teenage girl in the skimpy top,
   her boyfriend with three tattoos,
the truck driver traversing the country,
the physical therapist and
   the stroke victim she works with,
the lawyer, the fisherman, the cop,
the young actress clutching her Oscar,
the general with a chest full of medals,
and I writing this poem,
   and you reading it—
all, all wear this invisible warning:
FRAGILE! HANDLE WITH CARE!

In his book *The Friendship Game*, Father Andrew Greeley writes, "The need for tenderness is grounded in the vulnerability and fragility of human nature." We humans hurt easily. Unlike the rhinoceros and some other animals, we have no armor plate or thick skin to protect us. Quite the contrary, we are "both physically and psychologically vulnerable." How important it is for us to be aware of our own weakness, so we can respond in kindness to others.

For reflection

1. What does the first sentence of this poem mean to you?

2. Some people wear their "fragility" openly: a little child, an elderly woman with a walker, a foreigner struggling to learn the language of his new country, a young woman dying of cancer. But can you think of some individuals who may appear to be unbreakable, but are really fragile?

Suggested Scripture

LUKE 16:19–25
Lazarus and the rich man

2 CORINTHIANS 4:7–18
Earthen vessels

For prayer and play

Find a copy of the poem "Kindness" by Naomi Shihab Nye. (It can be found in her book *Words Under the Words* and in *Ten Poems to Open Your Heart* by Roger Housden.) Read the poem prayerfully. Or head a paper with the words "Kindness is…" and come up with at least ten specific examples of kindness.

50. When God calls you by name

When God calls you by name,
   don't look up and say, "Who, me?"
Worse yet, never say, "Here I am, Lord."

In fact, don't say anything at all.
Just go on doing whatever
   you were doing when he called:
     tending sheep, threshing wheat,
     washing dishes, jogging in the park.
Pretend you didn't hear him.

Then, when he's not looking,
   go hide under something,
     a bush, a bruised ego, bustle, bitterness.
Or better yet, run for your life!

Trust me:
somewhere in the vastness of the sea
is a whale ready and eager
   to give you asylum
     in the cavernous walls of his dank belly.

The Bible is filled with stories of men and women who were called by God: Abraham, Samuel, Gideon, Moses, Ruth, Jonah, Jeremiah, Isaiah, Mary. All responded positively—albeit some (like Moses and Jonah) reluctantly. This poem hints at some of the dangerous consequences of answering God's call. It also vividly describes the consequences of running away.

For reflection

1. The poem lists some of the places we can hide from God: under "a bush, a bruised ego, bustle, bitterness." Have you ever hid under one of these? What could be some other hiding places from God?

2. What could the "cavernous walls" of the whale's belly symbolize in life?

Suggested Scripture

JONAH
   The story of a reluctant prophet

LUKE 1:26–38
   The Annunciation

For prayer and play

Retell the story of Jonah for children. Or after reflecting on the Annunciation, write a letter to Mary thanking her for her "yes" to God.

51. The world is charged with the snares of God

The world is charged
  with the snares of God:
a cluster of pansies,
  the cardinal's song,
milky white clouds
  against a blue-gray sky,
a child's question,
  a neighbor's need,
the closeness of a friend,
  the scent of pine,
and loss upon loss upon loss—
all designed to stop us in our tracks,
and to call us forth
from the tomb of certitude and
  self-absorption
into the airy vastness of
  wonder and love.

The Jesuit poet Gerard Manley Hopkins wrote these memorable words: "The world is charged with the grandeur of God." This poem echoes his words but focuses on some of the specific means by which God can snare us. These snares have the incredible power of calling us forth from death to life. Ironically, the snares of God bestow true freedom.

For reflection

1. Have you ever been caught by one of the snares of God listed in this poem?

2. How can certitude and self-absorption be like a "tomb"? How are wonder and love like an "airy vastness"?

Suggested Scripture

PSALM 103
 Praise of God's goodness

PHILIPPIANS 2:5–11
 The obedience of Christ

For prayer and play

Make a list of the "snares of God" that have helped bring you into the "airy vastness of wonder and love." Or, after reflecting on the passage from Philippians, ask Jesus, "Why did you become a human being and die for us?" What do you hear Jesus say?

52. You've got four grandparents

You've got four grandparents.
Even if you don't know them
   or they're already dead,
you've still got them.
Four people who contributed
to your genetic makeup:
   your bone structure, eye color,
   proclivity for music,
   susceptibility to heart disease,
   distaste for numbers,
   that rough nail on your left little pinkie.

And you've got eight great-grandparents.
The same principles apply,
all eight having had a hand
   in making you you.
Now let's carry this thing a little further.
Let's say ten generations back.
Did you know you have 1,024 great-great-
   great-great-great-great-great-great
      grandparents?

Unbelievable but true!

And every single one of them
was healthy enough
  and lived long enough
to mate and produce a child
who was also healthy enough
  and lived long enough
to mate and produce a child who was
    also…
well, you get the idea.

Now why am I telling you this?

First, your particular existence
is a matter of gratuitous good fortune.
Remember that.
Second, it's possible that
  the man you cut off in traffic
    this morning,
  the woman you called a witch,
  the guy in the news
    you've labeled your enemy,
are all, all related to you
  genetically.
Remember that too.

As a child I used to look at the black-and-white pictures of my ancestors in our family photo album. Later on I was curious as to why my grandparents left Bohemia as teenagers and came to the United States. What did my great-grandfathers do for a living? What genetic traits did I inherit from my mother's side? Where did my family name, Svoboda, come from? Are there any famous people in my ancestry? An interest in ancestry, as this poem suggests, can be a good thing. The further back we trace our roots, the more aware we become of our interconnectedness with others.

For reflection

1. When you read that you have 1,024 great-great-great-great-great-great-great-great grandparents, were you surprised? What effect does this fact have on you?

2. Do you agree that "your particular existence is a matter of gratuitous good fortune"? Why or why not?

Suggested Scripture

MATTHEW 1:1–17
  The genealogy of Jesus

HEBREWS 11:1–16
  Our ancestors in the faith

For prayer and play

Bring to prayer today your family photo album or a few pictures of your ancestors. What do you know about each person? What would you like to say to each one? Thank God for all your ancestors. Or do some research on your family history or family name. Visit a library, go online, or consult with a family member.

SUGGESTED SCRIPTURE REFERENCES

(the number refers to the number of the poem)

INDEX OF
THEMES AND TOPICS

(the number refers to the number of the poem)

ALSO BY
SR. MELANNIE SVOBODA

Just Because *Prayer-Poems to Delight the Heart*

These prayer-poems have the uncanny ability to put readers in the presence of the universal and eternal, thus connecting them with God, others, nature, and the entire world.

128 pages • **$12.95** • **order 957743** • **978-1-58595-774-3**

With the Dawn Rejoicing

A Christian Perspective on Pain and Suffering

This deeply spiritual exploration of pain offers encouragement for anyone dealing with suffering—whether physical, psychological, or spiritual. It is rooted in Scripture and real life and touches on the many ways pain affects our lives.

144 pages • **$12.95** • **order 956999** • **978-1-58595-699-9**

When the Rain Speaks *Celebrating God's Presence in Nature*

If mystics are people who see God in everything, this book will teach you how to become one. This is a wonderful spirituality book for adults of all ages and a gift book that will be cherished.

160 pages • **$12.95** • **order 956845** • **978-1-58595-684-5**

By the Way *100 Reflections on the Spiritual Life*

Sr. Melannie has a gift for finding the sacred in everyday experiences, and in these reflections, situated around the seasons of the year, she shares not only her experiences but also the spiritual insights she has gleaned from them.

128 pages • **$12.95** • **order 958306** • **978-1-58595-830-6**

When the Moon Slips Away *Rejoicing in Everyday Miracles*

Each of these beautiful meditations begins with a thought-provoking quotation, has questions for personal reflection and/or communal sharing, and offers a short prayer that flows from the reflection.

144 pages • **$12.95** • **order 957286** • **978-1-58595-728-6**

1-800-321-0411
www.23rdpublications.com

TWENTY
THIRD
PUBLICATIONS